# SOUL-TIES

## BREAKING THE
## TIES THAT
## BIND

# BY: R.C. BLAKES, JR.

SOUL-TIES: BREAKING THE TIES THAT BIND
Copyright ©2017 by R.C. Blakes, Jr.

ISBN: 978-0-9910868-6-3

Published by Untapped Potential Publishing
P.O. Box 84355 Houston, TX 77584

UNTAPPED POTENTIAL

# CONTENTS

INTRODUCTION     7

1. What Are Soul-Ties?     11

2. Why Soul-Ties Are Hard to Break     29

3. The Demonic Powers Behind
   Soul-Ties     43

4. Signs of a Sick Soul     59

5. The Restoration of the Soul     69

6. How to Break a Soul-Tie     77

7. The Pain of Purification From
   Soul-Ties     85

8. Purging the Residue of a Soul-Tie     101

A FINAL WORD     113

# INTRODUCTION

LET'S JUMP RIGHT TO IT! I was a young kid and older women introduced me to sex. This experience perverted my young life and steered me down a path of depravity. I developed relationship after relationship based on things that were far away from any righteous foundation.

As I lived, I discovered that many of the women I had these encounters with were living in my head, many years after the affairs. They were in my SOUL, and in some cases, I was in theirs. Have you ever had anyone living in your head?

This reality would constantly creep into every new relationship and sabotage its' success.

Why did my mind constantly revert back to old people and old experiences? Why was my history imposing itself upon my present and even assassinating my destiny?

At the time, I had no understanding of spiritual dynamics, and I had no concept of soul-ties. It does not matter if we are aware or ignorant; if we contact fire it will always burn us.

Ignorance is not bliss! Ignorance is dangerous and possibly fatal. I was in the grips of a demonic stronghold. I had developed soul-ties, and it took me many years to break free and to be my best self.

Over the years, I have dealt with hundreds of people who have gone through the same things I did. In some cases, my experiences have served to guide many through the treacherous waters of soul-ties. As you read this book, my prayer is that you, too, will find the freedom that others and I have attained.

R.C. Blakes, Jr.

# CHAPTER 1

# WHAT ARE SOUL-TIES?

The very term soul-tie carries a sense of spooky spirituality. Religious people become apprehensive and suspicious. The term soul-tie is not found in the Bible, but the principle and function of soul-ties are clearly there.

**A soul-tie is defined as a spiritual and emotional connection that ties one person's life to another.**

The Bible speaks of souls being knit together, becoming one flesh, etc.

For instance, the Bible says in 1 Samuel 18:1:

*And it came to pass, when he had made an end of speaking unto Saul, that the soul of Jonathan was knit with the soul of David, and Jonathan loved him as his own soul.*

Here we see the souls of Jonathan and David being knit together in brotherhood. This is an example of a righteous soul-tie instigated by the Holy Spirit. The connection was healthy for both and provided a foundation for righteousness in both parties.

We see another biblical example of an unrighteous soul-tie that cost a man of God his anointing and his life. The biblical character is Samson and the soul-tie was with Delilah.

In Judges 16:15-21 it states:

*And she (Delilah) said unto him, How canst thou say, I love thee, when thine heart is not with me? thou hast mocked me these three times, and hast not told me wherein thy great strength lieth. And it came to pass, when she pressed him daily with her words, and urged him, so that his soul was vexed unto death; That he told her all his heart, and said unto her, There hath not come a razor upon mine head; for I have been a Nazarite unto God from my mother's womb: if I be shaven, then my strength will go from me, and I shall become weak, and be like any other man. And when Delilah saw that he had told her all his heart, she sent and called for the lords of the Philistines, saying, Come up this once, for he hath shewed me all his heart. Then the lords of the Philistines came up unto her, and brought money in their hand. And she made him sleep upon her knees; and she called for a man, and she caused him to shave off the seven locks of his head; and she began to afflict him, and his strength went from him. And she said, The Philistines be upon thee, Samson. And he awoke out of his sleep, and said, I will go out as at other times before, and shake myself. And he wist not that the Lord was departed from him. But the Philistines took him, and put out his eyes, and brought him down to Gaza, and bound him with fetters of brass; and he did grind in the prison house.*

The strongest man in the world was taken out by a sexual soul-tie. This woman caused Samson to forsake his family, God, and his purpose. The Bible says that *she pressed him.* Soul-ties are always a controlling relationship of some kind. A soul-tie is a relationship that challenges your morals and destroys your principles.

## There Is An Ordained Soul-Tie Called Marriage.

Marriage is God's ordained tying of souls. A man and his wife are joined and become one in the eyes of God.

The Bible says in Genesis 2:24-25:

*Therefore shall a man leave his father and his mother, and shall cleave unto his wife: and they shall be one flesh. And they were both naked, the man and his wife, and were not ashamed.*

God intends for husbands to be tied to wives and vice versa. My wife and I are so connected we think the same thoughts. Sometimes it can become scary.

**When We Function In Intimate And Sexual Relations With People As Though We Are Husband And Wife; The Same Connection Takes Place From A Platform Of Sin.**

When God tied Adam and Eve together they had no shame. When we join ourselves, illegally, to people in sexual relationships, it produces shame, pain and often death.

**There Is More To Sex Than A Physical Act. Sex Opens Your Soul To The Person You're Involved With.**

Take a look at what 1 Corinthians 6:15-16 says:

*Know ye not that your bodies are the members of Christ? shall I then take the members of Christ, and make them the members of an harlot? God forbid. What? know ye not that he which is joined to an harlot is one body? for two, saith he, shall be one flesh.*

This passage is informing us that the sexual act actually ends in a union between the two parties. There's no such thing as casual sex. All sexual activity carries heavy spiritual, emotional and physical repercussions.

## When We Have Sex, There's A Spiritual Bond Created.

The soul-tie is so powerful that even when you are separated from the person, they live with you in *memories, scents, music and places*. The thought of the person leads to physical sensations, obsessive thoughts and irrational behavior. It was irrational for Samson to jeopardize his anointing for a loose, worldly woman, but he did.

**Many Can't Function Within Marriages Because They Have So Many Old Memories Of Former Lovers That They Get Lust Confused With Intimacy.**

The strength of the soul-tie is strongholds, which are demonic thought systems that perpetuate desires for and attractions to things that don't agree with God.

Listen to the Apostle Paul as he talks about strongholds. He says in 2 Corinthians 10:4-5: *For the weapons of our warfare are not carnal, but mighty through God to the pulling down of strongholds; Casting down imaginations, and every high thing that exalteth itself against the knowledge of God, and bringing into captivity every thought to the obedience of Christ.*

A stronghold is a fortress designed to keep what is in locked in and what would challenge it, out. A mental/spiritual stronghold locks certain people, desires, habits and experiences into your mindset while preventing the power of God from entering that area. As a consequence, a person can love God and still be bound in certain areas of life, due to the strongholds.

Paul testifies in his letter to the Roman church in Romans 7:18-21. He says:

*For I know that in me (that is, in my flesh,) dwelleth no good thing: for to will is present with me; but how to perform that which is good I find not. For the good that I would I do not: but the evil which I would not, that I do. Now if I do that I would not, it is no more I that do it, but sin that dwelleth in me. I find then a law, that, when I would do good, evil is present with me.*

Strongholds are where these soul-ties reside. They are protected by a certain thought system we have acquired through various ungodly experiences with another person. A soul-tie is an addiction of sorts.

## Intense Perverted Sexual Experiences Create An Emotional And Physical Marriage.

Even though the spirit of the person disagrees with certain behaviors and the intellect knows better, the person is still drawn into complying with the urge for a certain person. It's a soul-tie hiding behind a sexual stronghold that continues to bring the person back. The sexual experience becomes the hook in the jaw of the fish. It won't let them go.

There's a powerful passage in Proverbs 6:26-29. It says:

*For by means of a whorish woman a man is brought to a piece of bread: and the adulteress will hunt for the precious life. Can a man take fire in his bosom, and his clothes not be burned? Can one go upon hot coals and his feet not be burned? So he that goeth in to his neighbour's wife; whosoever toucheth her shall not be innocent.*

This brother was playing with fire and didn't know it. He was ultimately destroyed because he kept going back. He kept going back because he couldn't help himself.

Another verse of scripture declares:

*As a dog returneth to his vomit, so a fool returneth to his folly* (Proverbs 26:11).

Let's look deeper into the Apostle Paul's description of the sin nature in mankind. It happens to also be a perfect description of the kind of lunacy that accompanies an unholy soul-tie.

Let us read Romans 7:15-19 in the Amplified version of the Bible this time. It says:

*For I do not understand my own actions. I am baffled, bewildered. I do not practice or accomplish what I wish, but I do the very thing that I loathe which my moral instinct condemns. Now if I do habitually what is contrary to my desire, that means that I acknowledge and agree that the Law is good (morally excellent) and that I take sides with it. However, it is no longer I who do the deed, but the sin principle which is at home in me and has possession of me. For I know that nothing good dwells within me, that is, in my flesh. I can will what is right, but I cannot perform it. I have the intention and urge to do what is right, but no power to carry it out. For I fail to practice the good deeds I desire to do, but the evil deeds that I do not desire to do are what I am ever doing.*

Wow! When I read this, I could feel the words because I have been here. I have been in a place where one part of me wanted God and another part of me continued to be drawn to relationships and experiences that served nothing righteous.

Unholy soul-ties can draw a beaten and abused woman to the abuser for a lifetime. He's a man, under normal circumstances, she would hate and run from, but instead she runs to him. This is an unnatural affection.

The Bible says in 2 Timothy 3:3:

*Without natural affection, trucebreakers, false accusers, incontinent, fierce, despisers of those that are good.*

**Soul-ties are definitely unnatural affection.**

Another example of an unnatural affection would be the young boy who was molested by a man and grows up with homosexual tendencies. His behavior and sexual stronghold stems from the soul-tie between him and his abuser. The soul-tie has perverted his self-definition.

## In The Demonic World, Unholy Soul-Ties Can Serve As Conduits To Transfer Spirits.

The scripture says in Matthew 12:43-44: *When the unclean spirit is gone out of a man, he walketh through dry places, seeking rest, and findeth none. Then he saith, I will return into my house from whence I came out; and when he is come, he findeth it empty, swept, and garnished.*

The text makes it clear that demonic spirits are constantly seeking a place to rest in. This is why the Bible says, "Give no place to the devil".

When a person engages in an unrighteous relationship, they open themselves to the spiritual realities of the person they become intimate with.

## How Soul-Ties Are Formed:

### 1.EROTIC CONVERSATION OR SEXUAL INTERACTION FORMS SOUL-TIES

Pornography and phone sex are channels for the development of soul-ties. You get your mind locked in on the perversion of that erotica and won't be content with intimacy.

King Herod was manipulated by a sensual dance.

In Matthew 14:6-9 it says:

*But when Herod's birthday was kept, the daughter of Herodias danced before them, and pleased Herod. Whereupon he promised with an oath to give her whatsoever she would ask. And she, being before instructed of her mother, said, Give me here John Baptist's head in a charger. And the king was sorry: nevertheless for the oath's sake, and them which sat with him at meat, he commanded it to be given her.*

This foolish man was taken in by a belly dance. The sensuality of it caused him to offer anything. Soul-ties are developed in any sensual experience. Married people talking sensually on the phone with someone other than their spouses are cheating. There is an emotional marriage being developed which will ultimately lead to a physical encounter.

## 2. DEVELOPING CLOSE FRIENDSHIPS CREATE SOUL-TIES

**All Soul-Ties Are Not Sexual.**

We must always be careful whom we allow to get too close to us, even in friendship.
For instance, the word of God says,

*Make no friendship with an angry man; and with a furious man thou shalt not go: Lest thou learn his ways, and get a snare to thy soul* (Proverbs 22:24-25).

Again, King David and Jonathan had a good soul-tie as a result of a good friendship (1 Samuel 18:1); but, bad soul-ties can form from bad friend-ships as well. Idolizing somebody can cause a bad soul-tie. I have seen friendships that were ruled by manipulation and control.

## 3.DECLARATIONS OF DEVOTION DEVELOP SOUL-TIES

Making pointless and careless vows of commitment and agreements are spiritually binding. For instance, Numbers 30:2 says:

*If a man vow a vow unto the Lord, or swear an oath to bind his soul with a bond; he shall not break his word, he shall do according to all that proceedeth out of his mouth.*

When it comes out of your mouth, you are responsible to fulfill it. People often say things like: "I can't live without you" or "I can never love anyone else but you." All of this language is establishing a mental and spiritual stronghold. The words of our mouths can create a binding contract.

I believe this is the very reason Proverbs 21:23 says,

*Whoso keepeth his mouth and his tongue keepeth his soul from troubles.*

**When You Pledge Devotion, You Give Demonic Spirits Legal Access To Your Soul To Feed That Declared Devotion.**

# CHAPTER 2

# WHY ARE SOUL-TIES HARD TO BREAK?

Once again, in Proverbs 22:24-25, it says: *Make no friendship with an angry man; and with a furious man thou shalt not go: Lest thou learn his ways, and get a snare to thy soul.*

The text uses some vivid language when it says, "a snare to thy soul". According to The Complete Word Studies Dictionary, the meaning of the actual word speaks of *a snare, a trap, or bait.* The proper understanding of this Hebrew word is *the lure or bait placed in a hunter's trap.* From this sense comes the primary use of the term to mean *the snare itself.* It is used to signify a trap by which birds or beasts are captured (Amos 3:5), a moral pitfall (Prov. 18:7; 20:25), and anything that lures one to ruin and disaster.

The soul-tie is harder to break free from than a fish on a hook or a bird in the trap. Once you're hooked, you may have a lifelong struggle to break free. Soul-ties are hard to escape for a few reasons.

## 1. THE INDIVIDUAL'S WILL MUST BE TOTALLY AGAINST IT

This simply means that the person must sincerely want to be free from the illicit relationship in every part of their being. Quite often, we want freedom on one level and we are still hooked on another level. Freedom will require a symphony of agreement between all three levels of the person's being; spirit, mind and body.

**To Break A Soul-Tie Will Require: Conviction In The Spirit, Renewing Of The Mind, And The Crucifixion Of The Flesh. The Spirit, Mind And Body Must All Align In Agreement.**

There is a powerful passage found in 1 Thessalonians 5:23 which says,

*And the very God of peace sanctify you wholly; and I pray God your whole spirit and soul and body be preserved blameless unto the coming of our Lord Jesus Christ.*

He uses the word sanctify, which means to *be set apart for divine purpose.* To be wholly sanctified means, to be in a state where the spirit, mind and body are all set apart to God.

## The Entirety Of Your Being Must Align Under The Auspices Of God.

Your will must be set against the soul-tie. Many people say they want to break the soul-tie and simultaneously pull away from the people and things that encourage their liberation. We must always factor in the weakness of our flesh nature. One part can be all in and another part may be sabotaging the process.

Jesus put it best in Mark 14:38 when He said:

*Watch ye and pray, lest ye enter into temptation. The spirit truly is ready, but the flesh is weak.*

## Any Part Of Your Being That Yet Craves Darkness Has Not Been Surrendered To God.

The word says in 1 John 1:5:

*This then is the message which we have heard of him, and declare unto you, that God is light, and in him is no darkness at all.*

Within all of us there are these sinful tendencies, these perverted thoughts, and unrighteous habits that only serve to draw us back into bondage. This phenomenon is called an *iniquity.*

The psalmist writes in Psalm 51:5-6:

*Behold, I was shapen in iniquity; and in sin did my mother conceive me. Behold, thou desirest truth in the inward parts: and in the hidden part thou shalt make me to know wisdom.*

**An Iniquity Is A Sin That Is A Proclivity Of Your Fallen Nature. It Usually Resided In Your Forefathers.**

Certain soul-ties are rooted into our iniquity. This is why our spirits may say "No" and our flesh says "Yes". The mind (soul) is stuck in the middle.

## 2. SOMETIMES THE SOUL-TIE FULFILLS OTHER SUBCONSCIOUS NEEDS

The soul-tie is often difficult to break because the soul-tie may be satisfying other subsurface needs in the person's life. Just like drugs provide the addict with an escape; sometimes, bad relationships are doing something beneath the surface for an individual.

The addict may actually hate the drug, but he needs the relief it gives him from his reality. His need for the relief is greater than his will to kick the habit.

**There Are Some Relationships That Meet Perceived Needs That Subconsciously Outweigh The Desire To Break The Tie.**

Many women develop affairs with outside men because their husbands don't adore and honor them. They give sex for even a false sense of intimacy. Many times, men give money to prostitutes to fulfill their need to feel desired by a woman when the wife doesn't show up in that area. These realities are common in marriages.

Paul instructs the married couples in this way in 1 Corinthians 7:5:

*Defraud ye not one the other, except it be with consent for a time, that ye may give yourselves to fasting and prayer; and come together again, that Satan tempt you not for your incontinency.*

**Sometimes, The Root Of The Soul-Tie Is Selfishness. The Person Is Fulfilling Some Personal Deficiency.**

Common Needs Met Through Soul-Ties:

**A. The Need To Feel Superior**

Sometimes, the soul-tie is in how the person makes you feel. We all have subconscious needs that often stem from our flesh and actually make us vulnerable to manipulation. King Saul had a high need to feel superior.

The word of God records in 1 Samuel 18:7-9:

*And the women answered one another as they played, and said, Saul hath slain his thousands, and David his ten thousands. And Saul was very wroth, and the saying displeased him; and he said, They have ascribed unto David ten thousands, and to me they have ascribed but thousands: and what can he have more but the kingdom? And Saul eyed David from that day and forward.*

We see a need in King Saul to feel superior. As a consequence, Saul may have easily been attracted to anyone that made him feel superior. A person with an over-inflated ego may develop a soul-tie with a flatterer and may be manipulated by words. In the meantime, the flatterer has a need to control.

## B. The Need To Feel Desired

This is a big one for ladies. Women have a need to feel desired. The reality is this: she may develop a soul-tie with a man that feeds this need and depletes every other aspect of her life.

There is a passage of scripture that captures the essence of this point. In Proverbs 7:18-22 it says:

*Come, let us take our fill of love until the morning: let us solace ourselves with loves. For the good man is not at home, he is gone a long journey: He hath taken a bag of money with him, and will come home at the day appointed. With her much fair speech she caused him to yield, with the flattering of her lips she forced him. He goeth after her straightway, as an ox goeth to the slaughter, or as a fool to the correction of the stocks.*

This loose woman took advantage of this man's weakness to be desired by a beautiful woman. Sometimes the soul-tie is hard to break because the need to feel wanted is so great.

## C. The Need To Not Be Alone

A big issue for many people is the need to not be by themselves. Some soul-ties seem indestructible, and it is because one party cannot fathom being alone. In John 4:16-18, the word of God says:

*Jesus saith unto her, Go, call thy husband, and come hither. The woman answered and said, I have no husband. Jesus said unto her, Thou hast well said, I have no husband: For thou hast had five husbands; and he whom thou now hast is not thy husband: in that saidst thou truly.*

This lady had five different men and none of them married her, apparently. Why? She clearly just needed somebody present. Many people are stuck in soul-ties because they view it as being better than being alone.

## 3. THE INDIVIDUAL HAS TO OVERCOME THE CHALLENGE OF TRANSPARENCY

Another reason the soul-tie is very difficult to break is because it may only be eliminated under the light of transparency. One may not hide a soul-tie and purge it simultaneously. To heal a soul-tie will require revealing it. NOBODY WANTS TO BE HONEST ABOUT THEIR OWN FLAWS!

The Bible puts it this way in Proverbs 28:13:

*He that covereth his sins shall not prosper: but whoso confesseth and forsaketh them shall have mercy.*

# You Can't Destroy A Soul-Tie In The Dark!

The way to freedom from soul-ties is complete honesty and full disclosure. The revolution must be televised for the whole world to see. The scripture teaches in John 3:19-21:

*And this is the condemnation, that light is come into the world, and men loved darkness rather than light, because their deeds were evil. For every one that doeth evil hateth the light, neither cometh to the light, lest his deeds should be reproved. But he that doeth truth cometh to the light, that his deeds may be made manifest, that they are wrought in God.*

The scripture declares that he who comes to the light shall be changed. The person that overcomes the shame and comes to the light will experience transformation.

# CHAPTER 3

# THE DEMONIC POWERS BEHIND SOUL-TIES

The thing we conveniently dismiss is the demonic aspect of soul-ties. This is the age of imbalance; we either don't believe in demons or EVERYTHING IS A DEMON!

The reality is that demons are very real, and they play a significant role in all oppression and torment. Many of these ties are so severe because there are demonic forces instigating the attachments.

**Soul-Ties Are Most Often The Consequence Of Rebellion Against The Holy Spirit, Parental Advice, Counsel Of Pastors, And Even Against One's Own Conscience.**

When relationships are born out of rebellion, there are spiritual consequences.

God reveals a powerful spiritual truth in 1 Samuel 15:23. It says:

*For rebellion is as the sin of witchcraft, and stubbornness is as iniquity and idolatry. Because thou hast rejected the word of the Lord, he hath also rejected thee from being king.*

Most soul-ties are the consequence of somebody knowing that this is not the will of God and continuing anyway to gratify the flesh. At the end of the day, they removed the divine covering over their life to flow in rebellion (witchcraft). Samson connected with Delilah against his parents' wishes. David rebelled against God and slept with Bathsheba. Solomon entertained women worldwide and their pagan religions against the admonishments of God. Soul-ties quite often start on a foundation of rebellion.

**Anything Produced Of Rebellion Opens Satanic Doors.**

A soul-tie is an open door to the spirit realm. When we perform the illicit actions that create the bond, they simultaneously open the door for spirits that set up in the soul to perpetuate the bondage.

## The Soul-Tie Is Empowered By Demonic Powers Intending To Destroy Your Future.

Quite often the people individuals are tied to are not as appealing as others they had gotten over easily. The soul-tie is different because of the spiritual element. There's a spiritual connector that introduces a demonic influence.

In my book, *THE FATHER DAUGHTER TALK*, I discuss how an ungodly man works to become a woman's emotional addiction. He intentionally creates a soul-tie the woman may never break free from. There are things that may be activated which authorize demonic powers to attach.

## 1. THE SPIRIT OF FLATTERY

Flattery is a drug. The need to feel desired and wanted creates an open gate to the soul. When a person fills that emptiness with flattery it becomes as a drug addiction that snares the individual.

**Flattery Defined**: *Excessive or insincere praise designed to deceive or use*

Listen to the words of the scripture found in Proverbs 7:15-23. It says:

*Therefore came I forth to meet thee, diligently to seek thy face, and I have found thee. I have decked my bed with coverings of tapestry, with carved works, with fine linen of Egypt. I have perfumed my bed with myrrh, aloes, and cinnamon. Come, let us take our fill of love until the morning: let us solace ourselves with loves. For the good man is not at home, he is gone a long journey: He hath taken a bag of money with him, and will come home at the day appointed. With her much fair speech she caused him to yield, with the flattering of her lips she forced him. He goeth after her straightway, as an ox goeth to the slaughter, or as a fool to the correction of the stocks; Till a dart strike through his liver; as a bird hasteth to the snare, and knoweth not that it is for his life.*

The demonic spirits of flattery and lust came together, to bring this man to his end. The man was under demonic influence and had no clue.

Even believers can be influenced by demonic powers when we live in our flesh!

**A Person That Struggles With Low Self-Esteem Is Hooked By The Spirit Of Flattery.**

## 2. THE SPIRIT OF MANIPULATION

The spirit of manipulation and control is a very active demonic force in soul-ties. When we open our souls to the wrong people, the spirit of control and manipulation can enter. We see this spirit quite often in ungodly friendships and abusive leadership in churches and the workplace. People feel helpless to the spirit of manipulation.

**Manipulation Causes Irrational Behavior And Out Of Character Decisions.**

The queen of manipulation and control was Jezebel. In 1 Kings 19:1-3, we find an interesting record concerning Jezebel and Elijah the prophet. It says:

*And Ahab told Jezebel all that Elijah had done, and withal how he had slain all the prophets with the sword. Then Jezebel sent a messenger unto Elijah, saying, So let the gods do to me, and more also, if I make not thy life as the life of one of them by tomorrow about this time. And when he saw that, he arose, and went for his life, and came to Beersheba, which belongeth to Judah, and left his servant there.*

The very name Jezebel literally translates as "WITHOUT COHABITATION". This spirit will never live with anyone it does not control or manipulate. This person intentionally positions you for manipulation. Everything is calculated to maintain an influence over you even when they are gone.

**Manipulation Impacts Emotions And Decisions From A Distance.**

## 3. THE SPIRIT OF CO-DEPENDENCY

Co-dependency is a spirit that entangles you to the point you feel as though you can't survive without this person or they won't survive without you.

**The Individual Will Meet Certain Emotional And/Or Physical Needs, And The Person Begins To Look To Them As They Should Only Look To God.**

The Bible warns us of allowing men to occupy a place in our consciousness that only belongs to God. For instance, the scripture declares in Proverbs 29:25-26:

*The fear of man bringeth a snare: but whoso putteth his trust in the Lord shall be safe. Many seek the ruler's favor; but every man's judgment cometh from the Lord.*

There's no man worthy of fear. Your source is God and He alone.

## The Demonic Force Plants The Lie That You'll Never Survive Without A Certain Individual.

The scripture puts it as plainly as possible. In Psalm 27:1-2 it says:

*The Lord is my light and my salvation; whom shall I fear? the Lord is the strength of my life; of whom shall I be afraid? When the wicked, even mine enemies and my foes, came upon me to eat up my flesh, they stumbled and fell.*

The spirit of co-dependency desires to shift the focus from God to man. It is in that deception that this demonic spirit causes one to make a god of another.

There's a biblical character that symbolizes the mentality of one oppressed by a spirit of co-dependency. He's found in John 5:7-8. It's the record of the lame man by the pool of Bethesda. He lay there for many years without any change. John 5:7-8 says:

*The impotent man answered him, Sir, I have no man, when the water is troubled, to put me into the pool: but while I am coming, another steppeth down before me. Jesus saith unto him, Rise, take up thy bed, and walk.*

Notice, he was waiting on somebody to help him to facilitate his deliverance. He was depending on people. When Jesus showed up He pointed the man to the power of God within the man himself. Everything he needed was always in him. *The God in you is enough!*

## 4. THE SPIRIT OF SEXUAL PERVERSION

Sexual perversion is a major demonic soul-tie. When a person pushes the limits sexually, they are tunneling into your soul.

### Every Illicit Sexual Encounter Has Demonic Undertones.

Sex impacts the body, the mind and the spirit. 1 Corinthians 6:18-20 says:

*Flee sexual immorality. Every sin that a man does is outside the body, but he who commits sexual immorality sins against his own body. Or do you not know that your body is the temple of the Holy Spirit who is in you, whom you have from God, and you are not your own? For you were bought at a price; therefore glorify God in your body and in your spirit, which are God's.*

Paul makes it clear that there is a connection between one's sexuality, morality and one's spirit. He shows us that sex impacts the body, the mind and the spirit of a person. SEX IS SPIRITUAL!

**Sexual Perversion Creates A False Sense Of Worthlessness And A False Sense Of God's Absence.**

This leads to a devaluing and a lowering of one's standards. Subconsciously, the person begins to believe that they are not worthy of anyone better than the soul-tie they are currently involved with. The woman with the five "common-law" husbands probably kept sleeping with the same kind of men because that's what she felt her worth was.

The demonic spirit will use the perverted act to create a deception of the individual as being worthless and God hating them for their actions. Neither is true; the person is not worthless and God does not hate them. GOD'S LOVE IS ENDLESS!

## The Spirit Of Perversion Destroys A Person's Capacity To See Their True Worth.

## 5. THE SPIRIT OF REJECTION

Emotional abuse such as rejection creates a psychological lock that often captivates the abused. It's the desire to prove one's self as good enough. It's about validation and the ongoing attachment is about closure.

## The Spirit Of Rejection Causes Us To Chase What's Running From Us. We Become Consumed With Proving That

## We Are Good Enough.

These things register on the surface as purely social and emotional. Quite often demonic forces keep us bound to the wrong people, just to avoid the pain of another rejection.

The truth is that we never need to live lives that are fearful of rejection. When men walk out, God always steps in. We don't need to maintain unhealthy relationships based on fear of rejection.

In Psalm 27:10, the Bible says:

*When my father and my mother forsake me, then the Lord will take me up.*

## We Must Never Give Place To The Influence Of A Spirit Of Rejection In Our Relationships.

# CHAPTER 4

# SIGNS OF A SICK SOUL

**A** soul-tie develops in a season when the soul is out of balance with the spirit. Man is a three-in-one being; he is spirit, soul and body.

The *SPIRIT* is the part of man that is divine. It is the part of man that is from God and responds to godliness. The *SOUL* is the will, mind, intellect and emotions. The soul is where choices and decisions are facilitated. The soul is the center of personality. The *BODY* is the house where the spirit and soul reside.

## When The SOUL Is Sick The Individual's Life Is Poisoned!

There is a remarkable passage of scripture found in Proverbs 4:23. In the Message Bible, the text reads as follows:

*Keep vigilant watch over your heart; that's where life starts.*

The term *heart* speaks of the internal parts of the person. If we don't take care of the spirit and the soul, the physical life will be negatively impacted. Soul-ties are the consequences of a soul out of balance.

**A Dysfunctional Soul Is A Soul That Is Disconnected From The Influence Of The Holy Spirit And Is Governed By Its Own Whims.**

The sick soul is "carnal" and is ruled by the desires of the flesh. The word of God refers to "carnality" as everything in man that is not under the control or dominion of the Holy Spirit.

**The Soul Must Be Protected Constantly.**

1 Peter 2:11 puts it this way:

*Dearly beloved, I beseech you as strangers and pilgrims, abstain from fleshly lusts, which war against the soul;*

The irony is that soul-ties are the consequence of sick souls, and sick souls strengthen the soul-ties.

**An Unholy Soul-Tie Disrupts The Divine Balance Of The Soul. It Makes One Irrational, Rebellious To God's Will, And Driven By Emotions.**

The healthy soul is submitted to the will of God spiritually, intellectually and emotionally. The word of God in I Thessalonians 5:23 says,

*And the very God of peace sanctify you wholly; and I pray God your whole spirit and soul and body*

*be preserved blameless unto the coming of our Lord Jesus Christ.*

There is no such thing as a healthy soul apart from submitting it to the word of God.

The Bible declares in James 1:21:

*Wherefore lay apart all filthiness and superfluity of naughtiness, and receive with meekness the engrafted word, which is able to save your souls.*

The soul is only renewed by intentionally baptizing it into the word of God. The word says in Hebrews 4:12-13:

*For the word of God is quick, and powerful, and sharper than any two-edged sword, piercing even to the dividing asunder of soul and spirit, and of the joints and marrow, and is a discerner of the thoughts and intents of the heart. Neither is there any creature that is not manifest in his sight: but all things are naked and opened unto the eyes of him with whom we have to do.*

# The Word Of God Exposes And Disposes Of Everything That Is Toxic In The Soul.

Signs That Your Soul Is Dysfunctional:

## 1. WHEN YOU DECIDE TO MOVE AWAY FROM THE KNOWN WILL OF GOD

Moving away from the principles of God's word is a clear indication that the soul is sick. In Romans 8:6-8, the Bible says:

*For to be carnally minded is death; but to be spiritually minded is life and peace. Because the carnal mind is enmity against God: for it is not subject to the law of God, neither indeed can be. So then they that are in the flesh cannot please God.*

The term *enmity* means that it is at war against. When your soul is sick, there will be an ongoing battle against the things of God. Hosea 4:6 says:

*My people are destroyed for lack of knowledge: because thou hast rejected knowledge, I will also reject thee, that thou shalt be no priest to me: seeing thou hast forgotten the law of thy God, I will also forget thy children.*

A sick soul rejects God.

## 2. WHEN YOU ARE CONSUMED WITH SOMEONE WHO DOES NOT AGREE WITH YOUR SPIRIT

Soul-ties become addictive relationships. You know that your soul is sick when you continue to return to a person that has done nothing but harm you.

The word of God says in Proverbs 26:11:

*As a dog returneth to his vomit, so a fool returneth to his folly.*

Bad relationships are like junk food; you know it's killing you, but you keep coming back for more. It's a relationship that hurts but you want it.

The Bible says in 2 Corinthians 6:14:

*Be ye not unequally yoked together with unbelievers: for what fellowship hath righteousness with unrighteousness? and what communion hath light with darkness?*

An unequal yoke is painful for the two animals involved. They are not on the same level and to join them will hurt at best and kill one or both at worse.

**An Unequal Yoke Is Represented In A Relationship That Hurts To Be In.**

## 3. YOU GET WHAT YOU DESIRED BUT YOU'RE ALWAYS MISERABLE

A sick soul is one that constantly pursues happiness and never finds it. The individual thinks they are going to be happy if a certain thing happens; and even when it happens, they are still miserable. They believe that a particular relation-ship will do it and that doesn't work. The soul is sick!

## 4. YOU FORSAKE AND HURT PEOPLE WHO HAVE BEEN LOYAL TO YOU

An ungodly soul-tie will cause the individual to become so confused they will betray the people who have been the most loyal to them. We see this demonstrated in the life of Judas, Jesus' betrayer.

The word records in Luke 22:47-48:

*And while he yet spake, behold a multitude, and he that was called Judas, one of the twelve, went before them, and drew near unto Jesus to kiss him. But Jesus said unto him, Judas, betrayest thou the Son of man with a kiss?*

When you read the complete story, you will see that Judas made an agreement with Jesus' enemies, and it ended in him betraying the Lord and Savior. Soul-ties can turn you into a traitor.

There's a powerful passage of scripture found in Psalm 41:9. It says:

*Yea, mine own familiar friend, in whom I trusted, which did eat of my bread, hath lifted up his heel against me.*

# CHAPTER 5

# THE RESTORATION OF THE SOUL

Soul-ties develop because the soul (mind, will and emotion) is out of spiritual balance. The only way the person may find liberty, in life, is to strengthen the soul. The soul must be built-up to break free.

I like the way the word of God puts it in 3 John 1:2. It states:

*Beloved, I wish above all things that thou mayest prosper and be in health, even as thy soul prospereth.*

The life prospers as the soul prospers. A sick soul will consistently produce a dysfunctional life.

### When The Soul Has Been Damaged, It Must Be Restored.

It is so beautifully stated in Psalm 23:3:

*He restoreth my soul: he leadeth me in the paths of righteousness for his name's sake.*

The psalmist says that God is a restorer of the soul. There are times when the soul must be renewed in the things of God.

How To Restore The Soul:

## 1.ACTIVATE SPIRITUAL ACCOUNTABILITY

There was an occasion when King David seemed oblivious to the condition of his soul until the prophet Nathan held him accountable. We will all do much better if we submit ourselves to spiritual authority.

The Holy Bible says in Hebrews 13:17:

*Obey them that have the rule over you, and submit yourselves: for they watch for your souls, as they that must give account, that they may do it with joy, and not with grief: for that is unprofitable for you.*

When we submit to spiritual authority and accountability, we allow others to watch for our souls. There are things we will be made aware of which we may be oblivious to at the time.

## 2. PRACTICE SPIRITUAL TRASH DISPOSAL

As the soul is being restored to the divine default, you will have to be mindful to discard of small, seemingly, insignificant thoughts as they arise. *I call this, weeding the soul.*

Just like a gardener has to pull the weeds on a regular basis, a wise person eliminates everything that could possibly prevent the best fruit from manifesting in his life.

2 Corinthians 10:4-5 states:

*For the weapons of our warfare are not carnal, but mighty through God to the pulling down of strongholds; Casting down imaginations, and every high thing that exalteth itself against the knowledge of God, and bringing into captivity every thought to the obedience of Christ.*

The individual must be mindful of everything that needs to be pulled down in his life.

## 3. MAINTAIN YOUR SPIRITUAL POSITIONING

To see a restoration of your soul will demand that you maintain your position. Instability is the cause of unnecessary dysfunction. Galatians 5:1 says:

*Stand fast therefore in the liberty wherewith Christ hath made us free, and be not entangled again with the yoke of bondage.*

Once you find a place of liberty, do not go back! Staying under the influence of the Holy Spirit is the main source of power for restoration.

## You Cannot Maintain A Healthy Soul Apart From The Holy Spirit.

The scripture declares in 2 Corinthians 3:17:

*Now the Lord is that Spirit: and where the Spirit of the Lord is, there is liberty.*

## 4. REVISIT YOUR INFLUENTIAL RELATIONSHIPS

If you show me your closest friends, I can show you your soul. You cannot have regular fellowship with a best friend that is a prisoner and not experience prison to some extent.

Show me your friends, and I will show you your soul.

Amos 3:3 says in the Message Bible:

*Do two people walk hand in hand if they aren't going to the same place?*

The Bible also says in Proverbs 13:20:

*He that walketh with wise men shall be wise: but a companion of fools shall be destroyed.*

## 5. MAINTAIN SELF-AWARENESS

In the process of restoring the soul, you must maintain a clear view of yourself. Do not allow self-deception to creep in. You should look at yourself with crystal clear honesty. Never lie to you about you. You can never adjust what you refuse to acknowledge.

The writer of Romans says in Romans 7:18: *For I know that in me (that is, in my flesh,) dwelleth no good thing: for to will is present with me; but how to perform that which is good I find not.*

When you know your condition, you then can figure out the necessary treatment. It is a sad person that ignores his own symptoms.

# CHAPTER 6

# HOW TO BREAK A SOUL-TIE

As I was pondering this thing called *"Soul-Ties"*, the Spirit of God began to give me some profound revelation. For spiritual matters, there is quite frequently a natural process to execute that may produce the change we need.

As I prayed about this most common struggle within the Body of Christ and humanity at large, God gave me a four-point approach to uprooting soul-ties: Repent, Remove, Renounce and Renew. These four steps capsulize the process of uprooting soul-ties.

## 1. REPENT

If any sins were committed to cause this soul-tie, on our part, we start by repenting of them. For instance, fornication is perhaps one of the most common ways to create nasty soul-ties.

# When We Have Engaged In Any Behavior That Has Fed The Soul-Tie, It Is Necessary To Repent Immediately And Turn Our Backs On It.

God's word says in 1 John 1:8-10:

*If we say that we have no sin, we deceive ourselves, and the truth is not in us. If we confess our sins, he is faithful and just to forgive us our sins, and to cleanse us from all unrighteousness. If we say that we have not sinned, we make him a liar, and his word is not in us.*

## Repentance Puts All Of The Works Of Darkness In The Light Of God's Truth.

The scripture says in 1 John 1:7:
*But if we walk in the light, as he is in the light,*

79

*we have fellowship one with another, and the blood of Jesus Christ his Son cleanseth us from all sin.*

A major part of repenting is redirecting our thinking in a godly direction through the word. James 1:21 puts it this way:

*Wherefore lay apart all filthiness and superfluity of naughtiness, and receive with meekness the engrafted word, which is able to save your souls.*

## 2. REMOVE

Many soul-ties live within physical objects. Every time the person revisits particular objects like old pictures, shared music, and even gifts received, the soul-tie is tightened. These objects symbolize the ungodly relationship, and can hold a soul-tie in place.

Check out the wisdom of the word of God in Hebrews 12:1. It says:

*Wherefore seeing we also are compassed about with so great a cloud of witnesses, let us lay aside every weight, and the sin which doth so easily beset us, and let us run with patience the race that is set before us.*

What might be the things that are besetting you? Items such as flowers and love letters, given during adultery, should be destroyed.

The Bible is not unclear on this point. In 2 Corinthians 6:17 it says:

*Wherefore come out from among them, and be ye separate, saith the Lord, and touch not the unclean thing; and I will receive you.*

Choosing to put distance between you and the things that feed your passion is critical. This is why the Bible says in James 4:7-8:

*Submit yourselves therefore to God. Resist the devil, and he will flee from you. Draw nigh to God, and he will draw nigh to you. Cleanse your hands, ye sinners; and purify your hearts, ye double minded.*

The text talks about resisting the devil. You will never break out until you are willing to remove certain things from you and you from certain things.

## 3. RENOUNCE

To renounce is defined as:

*(a)To give up (a title or possession, for example), especially by formal announcement. (b) To decide or declare that one will no longer adhere to (a belief or position); reject. (c) To decide or declare that one will no longer engage in (a practice) or use (something): renounce violence. See Synonyms at relinquish. To disclaim one's association with (a person or country, for example).* (The Free Dictionary by Farlex)

The person must verbally articulate a disdain and disassociation from the things, activities, and people that they once esteemed as wanted and needful. The same tongue that spoke vows of loyalty and desire must now speak against everything that facilitates bondage. We renounce with our words.

In Proverbs 18:21 it says:
*Death and life are in the power of the tongue.*

The word of God also declares in Matthew 12:37:
*For by thy words thou shalt be justified, and by thy words thou shalt be condemned.*

## 4. RENEW

The concept of renewal is not without clarity. Your thinking must be refreshed and renewed. You can't demolish a soul-tie with the same mental framework.

The Bible says in Romans 12:1-2:

*I beseech you therefore, brethren, by the mercies of God, that ye present your bodies a living sacrifice, holy, acceptable unto God, which is your reasonable service. And be not conformed to this world: but be ye transformed by the renewing of your mind, that ye may prove what is that good, and acceptable, and perfect, will of God.*

Renew means to renovate the thinking. This is the process of deliverance. This is not far removed from the physical experience of renovating a home; there must be the tearing out of the old material and replacing it with new material.

The renewing of the mind begins the solid work to uproot the strongholds that serve to solidify the soul-ties. When we challenge the thinking, we challenge the behavior. When we renew the mind, we reform the life.

# CHAPTER 7

# THE PAIN
# OF
# PURIFICATION
# FROM
# SOUL-TIES

**A** soul-tie is a stain on the psyche that must be cleansed. To cleanse the soul from this demonic influence is not a comfortable experience. To detach from this spirit of manipulation will be painful.

The scripture says in Psalm 119:71

*It is good for me that I have been afflicted; that I might learn thy statutes.*

There are some things we cannot learn apart from pain. There are some spiritual realities that will only manifest through the crucifixion of the flesh. *The purging of a soul-tie hurts.*

**There Are Times That The Heart Must Be Allowed To Break To Correct The Soul.**

Romans 8:13 says:

*For if ye live after the flesh, ye shall die: but if ye through the Spirit, do mortify the deeds of the body, ye shall live.*

According to the Complete Word Study Bible, the term *mortify* is the Greek word *"thanatoo"*. Its meaning is *to put to death by the intervention of others.*

I found this definition of *mortify* interesting when it said, "put to death by the intervention of others". What could it mean by "the intervention of others"?

In the case of the soul-tie, you must step out of the soul (mind) and by the will of your spirit crucify the will of your soul (mind). One part of your being has to check another part of yourself. Your spirit crucifies your carnal mind.

## The Flesh Must Be Crucified
## To Renew The Mind.

As the word of God declares in Romans 12:1-2:

*I beseech you therefore, brethren, by the mercies of God, that ye present your bodies a living sacrifice, holy, acceptable unto God, which is your reasonable service. And be not conformed to this world: but be ye transformed by the renewing of your mind, that ye may prove what is that good, and acceptable, and perfect, will of God.*

The renewing of the mind is the major part of making the body a servant to the will of God. To bring the body (behavior) into alignment with the will of God is only accomplished when the mind is renewed. The mind must be aggressively managed. All of this is painful on many levels when purifying a soul-tie.

## 1. THE PAIN OF CLARITY

Sometimes, the pride of hating to admit you made such a blunder connects you to the situation. You try to make it right and you try to make it work because it hurts to accept the failure. This is often the basis of bad relationships going on for many years. The person knew better a long time before but didn't want to face the pain of failure.

**You Can't Be Delivered Or Correct Something You Will Not Acknowledge.**

David didn't even recognize he had a soul-tie until Nathan confronted him. David had an adulterous relationship that led to murder and conspiracy, and he was clueless. Could it be that the pain of the truth provided for David a mental block?

Let's look at the confrontation between Nathan and David as it is recorded in 2 Samuel 12:7-10. It says:

*And Nathan said to David, Thou art the man. Thus saith the Lord God of Israel, I anointed thee king over Israel, and I delivered thee out of the hand of Saul; And I gave thee thy master's house, and thy master's wives into thy bosom, and gave thee the house of Israel and of Judah; and if that had been too little, I would moreover have given unto thee such and such things. Wherefore hast thou despised the commandment of the Lord, to do evil in his sight? thou hast killed Uriah the Hittite with the sword, and hast taken his wife to be thy wife, and hast slain him with the sword of the children of Ammon. Now therefore the sword shall never depart from thine house; because thou hast despised me, and hast taken the wife of Uriah the Hittite to be thy wife.*

Nathan brought CLARITY! Soul-ties require a moment of clarity by any means necessary. When David realized how he had broken the heart of God, it broke David. David ran into the presence of God with a contrite heart.

**Clarity Will Always Break Our Hearts In The Direction Of God And Manifest God To Us.**

The word says in Psalm 34:18-19:
*The Lord is nigh unto them that are of a broken heart; and saveth such as be of a contrite spirit. Many are the afflictions of the righteous: but the Lord delivereth him out of them all.*

Brokenness always follows clarity. When Jesus broke the woman at the well free from her soul-ties He pushed the error of her ways front and center. Jesus forced her into a moment of clarity.

The word says in John 4:17-19:

*The woman answered and said, I have no husband. Jesus said unto her, Thou hast well said, I have no husband: For thou hast had five husbands; and he whom thou now hast is not thy husband: in that saidst thou truly. The woman saith unto him, Sir, I perceive that thou art a prophet.*

## The Word Of God Interrupts Our Regular Scheduled Thought Systems And Brings A Righteous Clarity.

The reason the clear and uncompromised declaration of God's word is so necessary is because the word brings clarity  like nothing else. The word hurts and heals all at the same time.

The scripture declares in James 1:22-25: *But be ye doers of the word, and not hearers only, deceiving your own selves. For if any be a hearer of the word, and not a doer, he is like unto a man beholding his natural face in a glass: For he beholdeth himself, and goeth his way, and straightway forgetteth what manner of man he was. But whoso looketh into the perfect law of liberty, and continueth therein, he being not a forgetful hearer, but a doer of the work, this man shall be blessed in his deed.*

The word of God provides a painful but necessary clarity.

## 2. THE PAIN OF DETACHMENT

When we construct these soul-ties, we create mental fortresses. Within these mental castles, the person is renting space in our heads. The creation of an impenetrable boundary is real; at least they feel impenetrable.

In other words, it may actually feel like you might die to be separated from certain people. The detachment often feels like one is dying! Nevertheless, there must be a detaching before there will be a purifying.

It is made so plain in 2 Corinthians 6:17. It says:

*Wherefore come out from among them, and be ye separate, saith the Lord, and touch not the unclean thing; and I will receive you.*

**Isolation Comes Before Elevation.**

The act of separating is on different levels and each level is more and more uncomfortable. The person is detaching from what is familiar and sometimes convenient.

**There's The Pain Of Forsaking Compromising Environments.**

When breaking a soul-tie, you must consider the spiritual covering over your life and the daily environment you choose to be in. If you reside in a polluted house, it will be hard to avoid being polluted.

Isaiah 6:5 states:

*Then said I, Woe is me! for I am undone; because I am a man of unclean lips, and I dwell in the midst of a people of unclean lips: for mine eyes have seen the King, the Lord of hosts.*

Isaiah had a revelation of his own condition and the condition of his circle. To purify your life from the toxin of soul-ties will require changing company. The people in your life are either supporting or challenging your personal condition.

## There's The Pain Of Separating From Old Thought Systems.

The greatest challenge is to disconnect from the way we think. It's easier to back away from the chocolate cake than it is to forsake the very thoughts that tie us down. Changing the thinking is not always easy.

2 Corinthians 10:3-6 says:

*For though we walk in the flesh, we do not war after the flesh: (For the weapons of our warfare are not carnal, but mighty through God to the pulling down of strongholds;) Casting down imaginations, and every high thing that exalteth itself against the knowledge of God, and bringing into captivity every thought to the obedience of Christ; And having in a readiness to revenge all disobedience, when your obedience is fulfilled.*

We must recognize the thoughts that keep us tied down. It is then our personal responsibility to pull those thoughts out of our consciousness. As we purge the thoughts, we diminish the power of the soul-tie.

**A Soul-Tie Puts The Carnal Mind And Body In Agreement. The Objective Is To Make The Body And Mind Subject To The Spirit By Disconnecting Every Thought That Feeds The Unholy Alliance.**

## 3. THE PAIN OF RECONSTRUCTION

When a soul-tie is in place, the internal order is much like this: The mind and the flesh are in partnership against the will of the spirit. There's a part that truly desires to do what you know is right but you're powerless against it.

The Apostle Paul puts it in these terms in Romans 7:18-22:

*I realize that I don't have what it takes. I can will it, but I can't do it. I decide to do good, but I don't really do it; I decide not to do bad, but then I do it anyway. My decisions, such as they are, don't result in actions. Something has gone wrong deep within me and gets the better of me every time. It happens so regularly that it's predictable. The moment I decide to do good, sin is there to trip me up. I truly delight in God's commands* (Message Bible).

Paul said he couldn't do the good he desired and always manifested what he really did not desire. There was an internal arrangement of his being that worked against his righteous desire.

## There Has To Be A Reconstruction Of The Individual's Spiritual, Psychological And Physical Order.

Titus 3:5 says:

*Not by works of righteousness which we have done, but according to his mercy he saved us, by the washing of regeneration, and renewing of the Holy Ghost.*

According to the Complete Word Study Bible the term *renew* is the Greek word *anakainosis.* It means: *to renew qualitatively; to renovate the soul by the Holy Spirit.* It means *to renovate.*

# CHAPTER 8

# PURGING THE RESIDUE OF A SOUL-TIE

The maintenance of a broken soul-tie, in repair, will require lifelong intention. It's no different than a drug addict maintaining his sobriety. Soul-ties tend to tattoo the mind with impressions that invade the thoughts, stir the passions and even entice the flesh spontaneously.

There's a lot of residue that must be acknowledged as we move towards a life of freedom. There are areas of the personality that are strangled because of the trauma.

**Some Of The Consequences Of Soul-Ties Are: Low Self-Esteem, An Inability To Be Intimate With Another, And A Misguided Perspective On What Love Is.**

Ungodly soul-ties are sealed by demonic influence. When we entertain anything that is ungodly, we legalize demonic activity in our lives.

Ephesians 4:25-27 teaches:

*Wherefore putting away lying, speak every man truth with his neighbor: for we are members one of another. Be ye angry, and sin not: let not the sun go down upon your wrath: Neither give place to the devil.*

The greater principle is that behavior and choices which disagree with God, closes the door on the Holy Spirit and legally gives Satan a foothold in your life.

## For Instance, Fornication And Adultery Destroy The Intimacy Of Marriage.

Why do we have so many married people who are sexually frustrated? There are too many preconceived ideas about what is sexually fulfilling from previous acts of fornication or adultery. The soul-tie created through illicit sex incapacitates the intimacy of marriage. The residue of the soul-tie quite often is impaired intimacy.

## If We Adhere To God's Order Of One Man One Woman After Marriage, There Wouldn't Be Any Sexual Soul-Ties To Compare To Our Spouses.

The destruction of marital intimacy is only one example of the residue of soul-ties. This is probably an inexhaustible factor. Soul-tie residue is impacting relationships from the boardroom to the bedroom. When one has been impacted by a soul-tie and is now pursuing freedom he must be constantly aware of the residue.

How does one cleanse the soul of the residue behind a soul-tie?

## 1.FORGIVENESS IS A SPIRITUAL DETERGENT THAT PURGES THE RESIDUE OF SOUL-TIES

Quite often, we are focusing on fruit without ever addressing the actual root. When you are struggling with the residue of a soul-tie, quite often, you've not released the person who did you wrong. Unforgiveness actually marries you to the offender and your behavior is subconsciously dictated by that demonic marriage unawares.

The Message Bible puts it this way in John 20:23:

*If you forgive someone's sins, they're gone for good. If you don't forgive sins, what are you going to do with them?*

To hold on to someone's wrongs against you is like a spiritual warehouse of infractions. YOU ARE HOLDING THEM! YOU ARE CARRYING THE LOAD OF THEM! LET THEM GO!

**Most Soul-Ties Are Initiated Through Emotional Wounds And The Enemy Plants Seeds Into The Cracks Of Those Wounds.**

The most prolific text on this matter is probably Hebrews 12:15-16 which says:
*Looking diligently lest any man fail of the grace of God; lest any root of bitterness springing up trouble you, and thereby many be defiled. Lest there be any fornicator, or profane person, as Esau, who for one morsel of meat sold his birthright.*

In this passage we see that a root of bitterness causes defilement and unrighteous fruit. Notice he connects fornication to bitterness.

When we do not deal with the residue of the soul-tie, it may come up again in some other fashion. The bitterness was obviously the residue of some former infraction. The unprocessed residue evolved into fornication and other profanity. Any person that is recovering from a soul-tie experience must be cognizant of residue.

## 2. CRUCIFIXION OF THE FLESH PURGES THE RESIDUE OF SOUL-TIES

If we would continually stay on top of our sin nature it would force everything that does not originate with God out of our lives. Galatians 5:24 states:

*And they that are Christ's have crucified the flesh with the affections and lusts.*

## When We Crucify The Flesh We Drive Out All Defilement.

The impact of soul-ties and anything that is of the flesh becomes an involuntary reflex. HOLINESS is an intentional maneuver. There are some things that will have to be put off and others that will require putting on.

Romans 13:14 says:

*But put ye on the Lord Jesus Christ, and make not provision for the flesh, to fulfill the lusts thereof.*

When we make no place for the flesh, we simultaneously purge everything that is of the flesh. If you starve it, it will die.

**Fasting And Prayer Is A Spiritual Discipline That Is Specifically Designed To Purge The Soul Of Anything Anti-God.**

Jesus says in Matthew 17:20-21:

*And Jesus said unto them, Because of your unbelief: for verily I say unto you, If ye have faith as a grain of mustard seed, ye shall say unto this mountain, Remove hence to yonder place; and it shall remove; and nothing shall be impossible unto you. Howbeit this kind goeth not out but by prayer and fasting.*

There are some things that will only come out through consecration.

## What We Don't Consecrate Has The Potential To Desecrate.

## 3. OVERDOSING ON THE WORD OF GOD PURGES THE RESIDUE OF SOUL-TIES

The soul is a space that must be occupied, less the former tenants return. When we fill the soul with God's word, we drown out the voices of former influences and old bents (*tendencies*).

John 15:3-4 declares:

*Now ye are clean through the word which I have spoken unto you. Abide in me, and I in you. As the branch cannot bear fruit of itself, except it abide in the vine; no more can ye, except ye abide in me.*

Just like you made room for thoughts and feelings that didn't come from God, now you're going to have to become as fanatical about the things of God to purge your soul.

## 4. SURRENDERING YOURSELF TO THE HOLY SPIRIT IS THE ULTIMATE PURGING OF THE SOUL

If soul-ties are the consequence of demonic influence and sin, the Holy Spirit is the ultimate source of cleansing.

One of my favorite texts is found in Jude 1:24. It says:

*Now unto him that is able to keep you from falling, and to present you faultless before the presence of his glory with exceeding joy.*

The Holy Spirit is the agent of change and consecration in the life of a believer. Whenever something needs to be processed out of our lives, the Holy Spirit is necessary.

Learning to love the Holy Spirit and to fellowship with Him constantly is the only means of destroying and purging soul-ties.

Finally, Galatians 5:16-18 says:

*This I say then, Walk in the Spirit, and ye shall not fulfill the lust of the flesh. For the flesh lusteth against the Spirit, and the Spirit against the flesh: and these are contrary the one to the other: so that ye cannot do the things that ye would. But if ye be led of the Spirit, ye are not under the law.*

## WE CAN'T DO IT WITHOUT THE HOLY SPIRIT!

# FINAL WORD

I am standing in faith that you will break free from everything that binds you. It is the will of the Father that you would be free. I believe God for total deliverance of your soul from all unrighteous attachments. Pray this prayer with me please:

*Heavenly Father,*

*It is in the name of Jesus Christ, the Lord of Heaven and earth, that I come. I repent of every willful sin and even those that I may not be conscious of. Every door that I have opened to satanic influence I declare in the name of Jesus, THOSE DOORS ARE CLOSED! Satan has no right to influence any part of my life. I repent of rebellion, sexual acts, erotic conversations, participation in pornography, and even opening my life to any ungodly relationships of control and manipulation.*

*I declare, in the name of Jesus, MY SOUL IS COMPLETELY OCCUPIED with the Holy Spirit.*

*Holy Spirit, I now ask of You to fill my entire life; my spirit, my soul, and my body.*

*I repent for grieving You, and now, I totally surrender my whole life to You. Purge my conscience and my desires. Give me a holy frame of mind.*

*I forgive and release every person with whom I have engaged in unlawful relations. I repent of the wrong I did towards them, and I release them from any liability for the things they did to me. They no longer have any place in my soul. I am free from memories, feelings and desires. The blood of Jesus Christ washes my soul today. I AM FREE!*

*Amen!*

# ABOUT THE AUTHOR:

**R.C. Blakes, Jr.** is the co-pastor of New Home Family of Churches, a ministry consisting of multiple campuses between Louisiana and Texas. He is also the presiding Bishop of The Family of Churches Fellowship International (FOCFI; www FOCFI.org). FOCFI is an organization that provides spiritual covering for pastors, churches and five-fold ministry leaders.

He is the founder of The Father Daughter Talk movement which impacts the lives of fatherless women by teaching them the things every woman should have learned from her father about life and men. R.C. is also the author of The Father Daughter Talk book (the most important conversation of a young woman's life). He has also authored "Queenology: *There's A Queen Inside Of You*"; "Wisdom For Women In Ministry"; "The Laws of Manifesting Your Vision"; and "God's Playbook For A Winning Family" (co-authored by his wife Lisa).

**R.C**. is a nationally sought after speaker in conferences and seminars. He makes regular appearances on television as an advocate for the disenfranchised and to teach the Word of God.

**He** has an uncommon passion to use his strength to lift the downtrodden and to encourage the forgotten. He has a special place in his heart for the advancement of women. He is received and respected nationally as a spiritual father to thousands.

**With** all of these roles, his greatest role is that of husband to Lisa Blakes, father to four, and is a grandfather.

For Additional Resources or to
Schedule the Author for Speaking
Engagements, Contact:

R. C. Blakes, Jr. Ministries
P.O. BOX 84355
PEARLAND, TX 77584

Phone: 504-569-8205
Website: www.rcblakes.com
Email: Rcblakesministries@gmail.com

You may also explore other resources
such as online courses by R.C. Blakes at
www.rcblakes.com